IMAGES
of America

MARION COUNTY

On the cover: TELEPHONE LINEMEN INSTALLING TELEPHONE LINES. Prospect telephone employees pose while installing telephone lines in the 1890s in southern Marion County. (Courtesy of the Marion County Historical Society.)

IMAGES

of America

MARION COUNTY

Stuart J. Koblentz and the Marion County Historical Society

ARCADIA
PUBLISHING

Published by Arcadia Publishing
Charleston, South Carolina

Library of Congress Catalog Card Number: 2007925816

For all general information contact Arcadia Publishing at:
Telephone 843-853-2070
Fax 843-853-0044
E-mail sales@arcadiapublishing.com
For customer service and orders:
Toll-Free 1-888-313-2665

Visit us on the Internet at www.arcadiapublishing.com

*In memory of our friend Gary Barnhart, a gentleman and a gentle man,
who loved Marion, its people, its history, and sharing what he knew
about our community with every fiber of his being.*

CONTENTS

ACKNOWLEDGMENTS

A book such as this is the result of many people who join together for a common purpose. I would first and foremost like to thank my editor, Melissa Basilone, and Arcadia Publishing for their efforts in bringing this book to print. The board of the Marion County Historical Society and its director Gale Martin also deserve recognition for supporting this project and for access to the collection of photographs that the society maintains. The Marion Community Foundation also played a role in this project by providing the funds by which the modern digital imaging equipment was acquired for use by historical societies in Marion County. Images for this book were provided through the generosity of Jim Anderson, Craig Barnhart (who allowed us access to the collection gathered by his late brother, Gary Barnhart), Kensel and Opal Clutter, Bob Cook, Mary Ellen Dune, Nancy Earl, Babette DuSang-Jones, Martha Harruff Chapman, Oliver Hamilton, Nancy Gracely, Mr. and Mrs. Fred Haas, Louise Haley, Dianna Hamm, Helen Kauffman, Scott Kelly, Bob Lucas, Zenabelle Messenger, Carroll Neidhart, Shelby Needham, Mike and Linda Perry, Rhea Poulster, Stephanie Sonnastine Schertzer, Trella Romine, Carol Robinson, Ed Schweinfurth, Don Underwood, Randy and Sandy Winland, and Dorothy Young. Bede Agner and Carrie Jones-Hutchman also arranged scanning sessions at the Marion Senior Center and Kingston Residence. Lynda Williams, archivist for Marion County Historical Society, allowed me to dig in the collection and get in her way—I hope that I did not make too much work for her. Grover Bridges also gets my best wishes for his helping me find time to get the narratives written. I would like to thank E Haley, my partner in life who not only supported me during the project, but also assisted in the scanning sessions in Marion. Finally I need to thank Bertie, our Jack Russell terrier, who at the ripe old age of 14 (98 in human years) would rather be outside playing, but was content to sit on my lap when writer's block visited itself upon me or curl herself up at my feet while I worked on the book.

FOREWORD

Following the publication of *Marion*, I was asked by those buying the book when another book about Marion would be written. In your hand, you hold the book that was an outcome of those requests.

It was decided that since the city of Marion had dominated the first book, that this work would focus on Marion County and its rural communities. Over the months, I have learned a great deal more about Marion County than I knew about it going into the project. And therein lays the purpose of this work, to share some of what makes Marion County one of the best places to live and be from and, at the same time, whet the appetite of the readers of this book to go on and learn more about this place we call home. Education and learning are two of the greatest gifts that we can give to ourselves and those around us. Our willingness to learn and seek knowledge on things that we know little about is what separates us from the lower forms of life on this planet. As the old adage goes, if a tree is not growing, it is dying, and so it is with learning and sharing the joy of our discovery with others.

In reviewing this work, we tried to find images that have been previously unpublished. Where images have been reused, I have tried to provide more information about what is going on in the image than was previously shared in other works. We did have difficulty with finding historical images in some portions of the community. Now that this area has been identified, we at the Marion County Historical Society will work toward forming a better and stronger collection in those areas.

We also opted to cover three additional topics, Marion By Air, Jim Thorpe—the Oorang Years, and Shovel City, a look back the heyday of the steam shovel industry that started in Marion. Even for those who are not from Marion, these chapters should prove enlightening and broaden their knowledge on this area.

I would also ask that each reader take a moment to review the names listed on the acknowledgement page. The people listed on that page represent the real heroes of history in our community through their time and effort to make this book a reality.

Before proceeding with *Marion County*, it would do the reader well to have a baseline knowledge of Marion County.

Marion County is comprised of 406 square miles of land in north-central Ohio. Our county seat, also named Marion, is approximately 45 miles northwest of the state capital of Columbus. Marion County was erected by the Ohio legislature on February 20, 1820, and separated from its parent county, Delaware County, on December 15, 1823. The county is comprised of 15 townships that contain both informal and formally organized villages. Marion County was named for Gen. Francis Marion, also known as the Swamp Fox for his cunning escapades during the Revolutionary War.

In closing, thank you for taking the time out of your day to learn more about or reminisce about this place that we call home.

One

THE MARION COUNTY OHIO COURTHOUSE

The current Marion County Courthouse was built in 1884. The eclectically styled building has many elements that follow the Italian Renaissance School of architecture, especially the building's third-story balconies. Built of sandstone, the courthouse is crowned by an ornate clock and bell tower, itself crowned with a statue of Justice, sword in one hand and scales of equality in the other. Surrounding the exterior of the building, carved faces of mankind were placed as a reminder of how people have evolved and that government serves the needs of the common citizen.

Over the years, the courthouse has been enlarged and modified. The most notable exterior modification was the removal of the two exterior grand staircases, which occurred before World War II. In the 1970s, the interior of the courthouse was "remuddled," a process that enclosed the grand staircase and removed some of the dignity from the interior of the building. Another unplanned modification was the temporary disappearance of the statue of Justice (also known as Lady Justice) in the early 1950s. Removed during maintenance, the statue was left resting upon the courthouse property one evening and gone the following morning. For almost 30 years, the whereabouts of the statue remained a mystery, wrapped in a riddle, surrounded by speculation. She was eventually returned, refurbished, and restored to her proper place atop the courthouse. County offices have been relocated to the administration building on West Center Street. Still the probate court, clerk of courts, and court of common pleas remain in this most historic structure.

The citizens of Marion County will soon decide on the fate of what is arguably Marion's largest community anchor and the proper seat of its courts. It is hard to imagine the community without this courthouse.

WATER TESTING, 1890. In order to protect Marion's structures, the fire department needed to ensure that the city water pressure was up to strength and that the equipment could handle this task. Because the courthouse was the tallest building at that time, both water and equipment needed to be proven effective and able to fight fires wherever they may occur. (Courtesy of the Marion County Historical Society.)

COURTROOM, 1895. Public buildings should inspire respect for the solemn proceedings that occur within their walls and in their chambers. Such was the design of the courtroom in the courthouse. (Courtesy of the Marion County Historical Society.)

10

WELCOME, 1898. In a rare lighthearted moment, the courtroom was decorated to celebrate the New Year. The details of the event and the reason behind the appearance by the stuffed horse are not known. (Courtesy of the Marion County Historical Society.)

SOUTH FACADE, 1909. While the Main Street facade of the courthouse is now accepted as the front of the building, the Center Street facade was at one time an entrance to the building as well. This entrance and staircase were removed before World War II to make more space inside the building for officials. (Courtesy of the Marion County Historical Society.)

PRESIDENT TAFT ADDRESSES MARION. Following his loss in 1912 to Woodrow Wilson, former president William Howard Taft made a tour of several Ohio cities upon his arrival back in Ohio in the spring of 1913. Taft's speech was for the most part congenial. Taft did express, however, his dislike for Teddy Roosevelt, his predecessor in the White House whose third party, Bull Moose, had cost Taft the election. As fate would have it, when *Marion Star* publisher Warren G. Harding was elected 29th president in 1920, one of most successful appointments made by Harding was nominating Taft to the position of chief justice of the Supreme Court. Those studying the history of the Supreme Court agree that Taft's best years in Washington were spent guiding the Supreme Court. (Courtesy of the Marion County Historical Society.)

COMMUNITY CHRISTMAS TREE. Members of the Marion community gathered around the Christmas tree standing on the courthouse grounds. The excitement was over the lighting of the tree that season. (Courtesy of the Marion County Historical Society.)

HONOR ROLL, ABOUT 1945. A permanent honor roll was erected on the west side of the courthouse recognizing the men and women of the community who sacrificed their lives and served their country during World War II. The memorial stayed in place into the 1970s when it was removed. (Courtesy of the Marion County Historical Society.)

COURTHOUSE AND TAFT HOTEL. In 1966, the Marion County commissioners purchased the Taft Hotel (originally the Kerr House) for $66,000 with the intent of using the land to build a county administration building. (Courtesy of the Marion County Historical Society.)

RAZING THE TAFT HOTEL. This image shows the razing of the Taft Hotel in the late 1960s. The land was not used for its original purpose, but instead for a parking lot, with many of the spaces reserved for elected officials. (Courtesy of the Marion County Historical Society.)

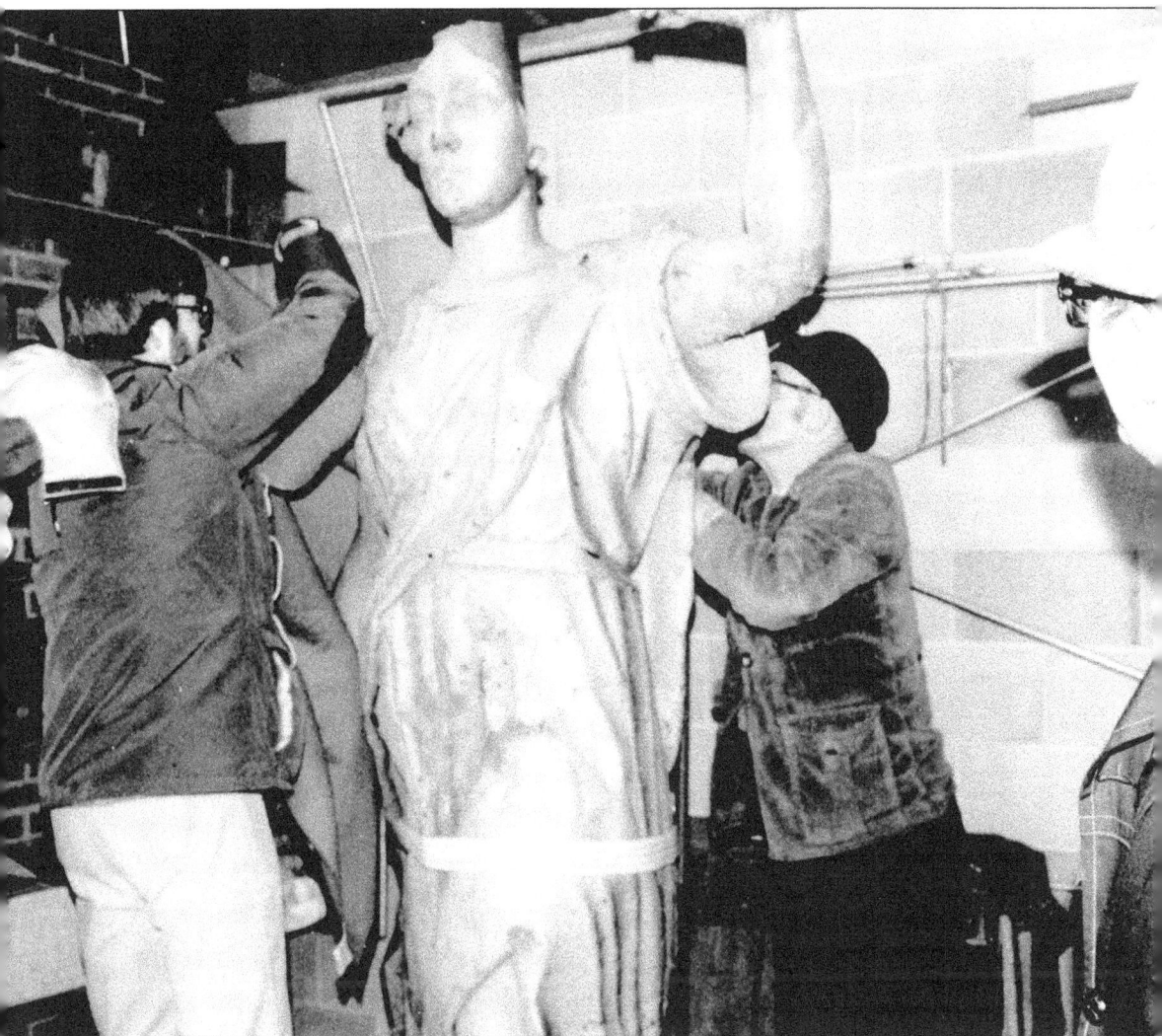

RETURN OF LADY JUSTICE. In 1980, Lady Justice was returned to the people of Marion County through the efforts of Charlie Evers and Carroll Neidhart. The statue, missing since the early 1950s, had been removed during maintenance of the courthouse clock tower. Once down on the ground, it was evident that almost 60 years of the elements had taken its toll on Lady Justice, who was missing her scales and sword, as well as part of her head. She was taken one night from the courthouse grounds, and community uproar afterward occurred while officials searched in vain for those responsible. In the 1970s, Evers again renewed the call to solve the mystery and return Lady Justice to her rightful owners, the people of Marion County. Finally a deal was brokered through an anonymous source, with Neidhart acting as the go-between. This photograph was taken at the unveiling in the WMRN garage on North Main Street. The statue was returned to whole and restored to its rightful place atop the courthouse. Officially the name or names of those involved have never been revealed—thus the mystery continues. (Courtesy of Trella Romine.)

CENTENNIAL CELEBRATION. On July 4, 1984, a centennial celebration was held in honor of the courthouse. Judge Charlton Myers addressed the crowd, speaking from the Center Street balcony, on behalf of the building that had served its community for 100 years to that point. (Courtesy of the Marion County Historical Society.)

OHIO HISTORICAL MARKER UNVEILING. An Ohio Historical Marker, placed on the south side of the building, was unveiled on the day of the centennial celebration. The marker details the rich heritage of the courthouse, a building that anchors the community and bridges the present with the past. (Courtesy of the Marion County Historical Society.)

Two

MARION FROM THE AIR

Like many communities, Marion County has grown and changed since its earliest days. In the era before photography, artist rendered drawings and paintings that helped to document the community. The advent of photography helped to advance the reliability of the documentation and the ease by which it could be made. Following the invention of air craft, aerial photography helped to further document the changes to a community by capturing views previously unseen. Many of the following images are part of the Marion County Historical Society's archive of commercial aerial photography and represent a small selection of the images available. All of the images in this chapter represent an ongoing photographic record of Marion and Marion County.

ADAM BAUER'S KITE PHOTOGRAPH. One of the earliest (1907) and most experimental aerial images of Marion was taken by photographer Adam Bauer using a kite to lift his camera up into the air. The image was taken from the area near Windsor Street on Marion's west side looking northeast toward downtown. (Courtesy of Mike and Linda Perry.)

INTERSECTION OF CHURCH AND STATE STREETS, ABOUT 1921. This image shows how the southeast section of downtown Marion, looking northwest, appeared. The large building in the center left is the U.S. post office (now Heritage Hall), and the large commercial block with the tower was the original YMCA building. The current location of Sky Bank on East Church Street was a filling station. (Courtesy of Craig Barnhart, Gary Barnhart collection.)

HARDING MEMORIAL, LOOKING SOUTH, ABOUT 1930. When selection for the Harding Memorial was made, the Harding Memorial Association chose the southeast corner of Vernon Heights Boulevard and U.S. Route 23 (Marion Waldo Road)—what had been the Uncapher Farm. The view beyond the Harding Memorial was one of open farm fields stretching to Waldo. Commercial development of the area would not begin until the late 1950s. (Courtesy of the Marion County Historical Society.)

MARION COUNTY FAIRGROUNDS, 1953. In 1944, the grandstand and racetrack at the Marion County Fairgrounds was selected by 20th Century Fox for the racing scenes in the movie *Home in Indiana*. Since that time, the biggest change to the fairgrounds was the addition of Veterans Memorial Coliseum in 1950. (Courtesy of the Marion County Historical Society.)

WEST CENTER STREET DOWNTOWN, 1957. West Center Street and downtown Marion were the hub of commerce and shopping in 1957 when this aerial image was taken. Most prominent in the image is the Hotel Harding. (Courtesy of the Marion County Historical Society.)

EAST CENTER STREET, 1957. East Center Street at Greenwood Street was a vibrant multiuse intersection in 1957 before the advent of the state-mandated one-way street system. The Isaly Dairy was in full production and busy with customers, as was Alber's Grocery Store across the street. The Seffner mansion to the left of Isaly Dairy was still standing, used as an apartment house. Hajjar's One-Hour Martinizing Drycleaners operated as a store built onto the front of what was once the largest house in the city of Marion. (Courtesy of the Marion County Historical Society.)

UNCAPHER FARMHOUSE AND SMITH CLINIC, 1961. The Uncapher farmhouse originally stood at the corner of Vernon Heights Boulevard and U.S. Route 23 (Marion-Waldo Road) on what would become the grounds of the Harding Memorial. In 1924, the structure was moved to a new location south of the memorial grounds and continued in its role as a residence until the property was purchased by the Smith Clinic, which built its new structure on the site. The Smith Clinic, founded by Dr. Frederick Smith, was the first modern medical practice in Marion, bringing together doctors from various fields of expertise. Smith's ultimate goal of opening a community-based hospital on the property that would serve any resident in need was realized soon after. The house was razed as the Smith Clinic enlarged its building. (Courtesy of the Marion County Historical Society.)

KENNEDY FORD AND EXECUTIVE PARK, 1972. Built on what was once the original site of Mar-O-Del Golf Course, Kennedy Ford joined the growing shift of businesses moving south in 1966. The move was driven by the construction of Marion General Hospital in 1953 and the development around the hospital of Executive Park and its medical offices. Next to Kennedy Ford is the LK Restaurant, one of the first modern commercial buildings built in the area; the LK Restaurant's corporate headquarters was built behind the restaurant building on Ellen Kay Drive. Holiday Inn opened its Marion location in 1964 on the corner of Executive Drive and Marion Waldo Road. (Courtesy of the Marion County Historical Society.)

HARDING MEMORIAL GROUNDS AND GENERAL TELEPHONE AND ELECTRIC. This 1972 image shows the Harding Memorial and its grounds as well as the General Telephone and Electric (GTE) of Ohio building. When designing what would become known as the "castle," GTE stated in the *Marion Star* that the facility's "park like" landscaping was planned to harmonize with the Harding Memorial's landscaping plan. Efforts to commercially redevelop the site have been met with resistance from the community, which would prefer that the "park like" grounds remain harmonized to the adjacent memorials. (Courtesy of the Marion County Historical Society.)

Three

GRAND PRAIRIE, SCOTT, AND TULLY TOWNSHIPS

Organized by 1824, Grand Prairie Township is part of the land acquired by the United States government from the Native Americans in 1819 known as the "New Purchase." It sits on the divide between the Ohio River and Great Lakes watersheds. The first church, an old school Baptist, was organized at John VanMeter's home in 1827. The first log schoolhouse was erected about 1832; Isaac James was the first teacher. Brush Ridge, another name that harkens back to the early days, is the township's largest crossroads community. The original prairie and woodland has been converted to productive farms.

Scott Township was named for Abraham Scott, a settler of 1821. It was detached from Canaan Township on March 5, 1822, upon petition by the settlers. Originally the land was partly wooded; a large portion of the land is on the Sandusky Plains, which was covered with water where maiden cane grew 15 to 20 feet high. The township contains several low-lying swales, two of which are the Wolf Pond and the Green Sea, which collect water. The Columbus Sandusky Pike provided access to the area, and Marturen Letimbra laid out Letimberville in 1833. Thomas Monnett kept the first store there. The name was changed to Kirkpatrick about 1910, it was named for a blacksmith in the village. Scott, along with Grand Prairie, Marion, and Claridon Townships, carried the brunt of the displacement caused by the Scioto Ordnance Plant from 1942 to 1945.

Tully Township was organized in 1828 from Scott Township. It was named by Alanson Packard for the township in New York State that was his former home. Tully Township is the sole remnant of Marion County's eastern tier of original townships, which were detached when Morrow County was formed in 1848. When four railroads (the Cleveland, Columbus, Cincinnatti and Indianapolis; the New York; the Pennsylvania and Ohio; and the Ohio Central) junctioned at a point within the township, a village grew up around the post office there. In August 1881, it was surveyed and laid out in 69 lots. The community was named Three Locusts because of the three large locust trees in the town. Later the community changed the name of the village to Martel. Tully City, across the tracks, was laid out by Dr. George. T. Harding (father of Warren G. Harding) and later became part of Martel.

BURTSFIELD RESIDENCE, 1885. Built in 1845, the John Burtsfield residence was originally designed in the "steamboat" Gothic style. Heavily altered since this photograph was taken, the house is located on Linn Hipsher Road, west of what is now U.S. Route 23. John Burtsfield is standing in the yard, his wife, Amanda, and daughters-in-law Neoma and Sabra Burtsfield are seated on the porch, as is granddaughter Florence. (Courtesy of the Marion County Historical Society.)

CHARLES PHILBROOK FARM, 1900. The Philbrook farm was located on Linn-Hipsher Road East and was originally settled by Mabel Philbrook's great-grandfather Abraham Lucas. Charles Philbrook farmed there until the land was taken for the Scioto Ordnance Plant in May 1942. (Courtesy of the Marion County Historical Society.)

DAVID HINAMON AND FAMILY. David Hinamon served as Grand Prairie Township trustee and elected Marion County commissioner, a position he held for many years. The Hinamon residence was located at Marseilles-Galion Road and State Route 4 across from the Hinamon Quarry, which is the longtime home of the Marion Fish and Game Association. (Courtesy of Kensel Clutter.)

ON THE VAN METER FARM, ABOUT 1900. Vern Lucas, Floyd Van Meter, and A. E. Lucas stand with four workhorses on the Van Meter Farmstead on Linn Hipsher Road. The image shows the size difference between the common horses on the left and the larger Percheron workhorses on the right side of the photograph. (Courtesy of the Lucas family.)

BREWER FAMILY AND RESIDENCE, 1907. The Edward Brewer residence was once located on Marion-Upper Sandusky Road. The house, which was one of the best examples of Carpenter Gothic architecture, burned after 1907. A complete loss, it was soon discovered that in one of the fireplaces was a grate of logs—completely untouched by the fire. (Courtesy of Kensel Clutter.)

BREWER BARN, 1907. Another architectural rarity, not just in Marion County but in Ohio as well, is the Brewer family barn, which is square with a true hip roof. Still standing, the barn has since had its copula removed and remains in the Brewer family. (Courtesy of Kensel Clutter.)

TO LAKE ERIE AND TO THE OHIO RIVER, 1909. Along Kenton-Galion Road, five miles northwest of Marion is the Divide. A house built at the crest of the hill, with its ridgeline perpendicular to the road, would shed water into two different water systems. To the south of the line, water flows into the Sandusky River system and Lake Erie; to the north of the line, water flows into the Scioto River system and is carried to the Ohio River. (Courtesy of Randy Winland.)

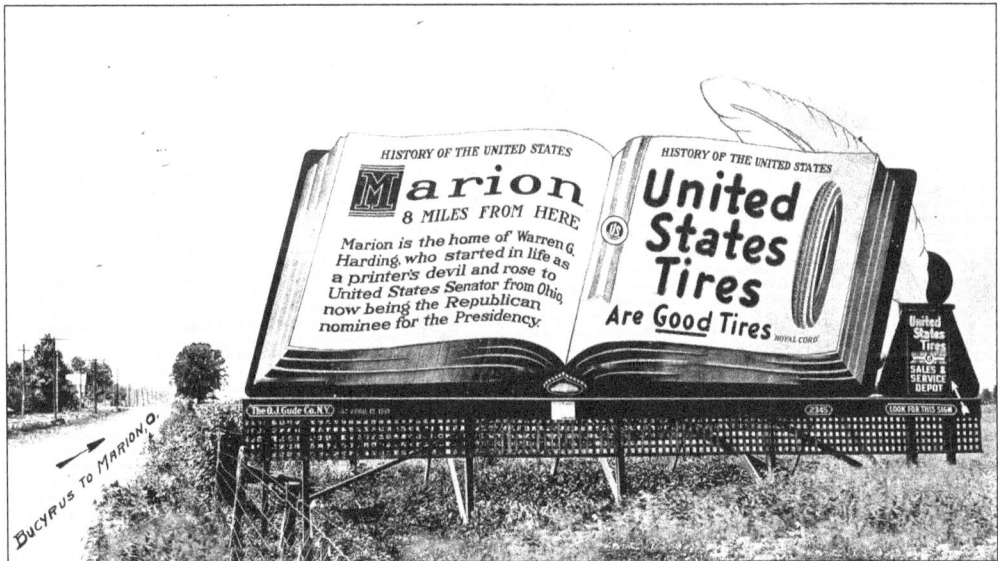

ALL ROADS LEAD TO MARION. This 1920 billboard was erected just north of Morral-Kirkpatrick Road and pointed the way to Marion where Warren G. Harding was campaigning to be elected 29th president of the United States. United States Tire would eventually become General Tire. (Courtesy of Craig Barnhart, Gary Barnhart collection.)

31

HARVEY STATION. This water tower once marked the location of Harvey Station, a local mail stop and siding owned by the Harvey family. Though no longer used to water steam engines, the tower is a well-known landmark in northern Marion County and is visible from U.S. Route 23. (Courtesy of Stuart J. Koblentz.)

LUCAS FAMILY REUNION, 1940. Members of the Lucas, Foos, Mason, and Burtsfield families gathered at the Mason Farm near Windy Corners for a family reunion in 1941. Within a year, each family would lose part or all of their livelihoods when their property was seized for the Scioto Ordnance Plant. (Courtesy of the Lucas family.)

PAUL CLUTTER, 1945. Paul Clutter was photographed by a factory representative using the latest technology for planting corn in this 1945 photograph. Note that his Allis Chalmers tractor is equipped with pneumatic tires. (Courtesy of Kensel Clutter.)

SONNANSTINE RESIDENCE, 1950. While one-floor houses are not new, Thomas and Mildred Sonnanstine's residence on Route 4 was considered thoroughly modern and different from anything else in Grand Prairie Township when it was built in 1950. (Courtesy of Stephanie Schertzer.)

KIRKPATRICK, 1909. Platted as Letimberville in 1834, and later named Kirkpatrick, one of the first businesses established an inn, which served travelers on the Columbus Sandusky Pike. The inn, seen on the right of this image, served liquor in the 1850s, a practice that was quickly put down by the temperate Methodist Episcopal women (wielding hatchets) who lived in the vicinity of the area. (Courtesy of Stuart J. Koblentz.)

BUZZARDS GLORY, ABOUT 1900. According to Kensel Clutter, this is an image of Buzzards Glory, south of Kirkpatrick on State Route 98. The name originated when the longtime owner, who raised sheep for wool and nothing else, allowed the bodies of the sheep that died in the field to rot in the field, attracting buzzards that feasted on the carcasses of the animals. (Courtesy of Kensel Clutter.)

THRESHING CREW AT REST. Threshers and their family members take a break while working at the Likins Farm near Kirkpatrick. During the harvest season, farmers would join together to help one another, many hands making for light work. Families would come along and prepare food for the men (and sometimes women) in the field. (Courtesy of Kensel Clutter.)

KID CART, 1902. Agnes and John Davids were given permission to hook up one of the older horses on their father's farm and take their handmade "kid cart" for a visit along the Iberia Pike, now Marseilles-Galion Road East. Along for the ride were the family dog and a lamb held in Agnes's arms. (Courtesy of Stuart J. Koblentz.)

BLACKSMITH SHOP. While Kirkpatrick never developed a strong business community, one profession in demand in the 19th and early-20th century was the blacksmith. Blacksmiths shoed horses, fixed chains, sharpened blades, and forged replacement parts for broken implements, leaving little time to rest beneath the spreading boughs of a chestnut, or any other type of tree. (Courtesy of Kensel Clutter.)

SHARP SCHOOL, SUB-DISTRICT 7. Students pose with their teacher, Mabel Rowe, outside their one-room school on Marseilles-Galion Road in 1905. Only the people in the back row in this image were recorded as Agnes Davids, Hazel Monnette, Miss Rowe, John Davids (in front of Miss Rowe), I. R. Monnette, and Darrell and Wayne Mitchell. (Courtesy of Stuart J. Koblentz.)

MONNETT FARM, 1912. Hazel Monnett and neighbors (listed from left to right) Carl Hill, Edgar Hill, and Lawrence Baker clown for the camera in the winter of 1911. The farmhouse was razed in the 1980s. (Courtesy of Kensel Clutter.)

ONWARD CHRISTIAN SOLDIERS. Members of the Kirkpatrick Chapter of the Women's Christian Temperance Union (WCTU) pose for this image taken about 1900. The unit was under the direction of Placidia Shaw, daughter of the local Methodist Episcopal minister. Each member wore a purple ribbon and carried a pike, symbolic of their crusade against rum and ruin. (Courtesy of Kathy Ferrell-Moore.)

KIRKPATRICK SCHOOL. Built in 1917 and closed in 1948, Kirkpatrick School, also known as "Kirk," was the one of the smallest centralized schools in Marion County. Classroom windows faced east. For a gymnasium, students used the township hall behind the school. While from a small school, the Kirk boys' and girls' basketball teams were fierce competitors and often won county championships. (Courtesy of Kensel Clutter.)

LIBERTY METHODIST EPISCOPAL CHURCH, 1940. Liberty Methodist Episcopal Church in Kirkpatrick was dedicated in June 1919. Congregation members purchased a Model T truck to haul materials to the site. The windows on either side of the front doors were carried over from the previous building and memorialize members of the Monnett family who led and supported the early settlement of the area by Liberty Methodist Church followers. (Courtesy of Kenzel Clutter.)

LIVING HIGH ON THE HOG, AROUND 1927. Barbara Brooks enjoys a moment in shade seated upon one of the hogs raised on the family farm. Though a resident of Dallas Township, Crawford County (immediately north of Scott Township), Barbara attended school and church in Kirkpatrick, immediately south of Brooks farm. (Courtesy of David Brooks.)

COUNTY CHAMPS, 1940. Members of the Kirkpatrick girls' basketball team carried a 10-0 record winning the 1940 Marion County championship trophy. Contact sports for girls ended in Marion County in 1940 over fears of potential "damage" to a young woman's health. First Lady Eleanor Roosevelt also lobbied nationally for an end to girls' contact sports because she found them "unladylike." (Courtesy of Stuart J. Koblentz.)

DOWNS CASH STORE. Martel was the largest community in Tully Township and provided community members with a variety of stores and services. Downs Cash Store carried a general line of merchandise but dealt exclusively with cash payments—no credit was offered. (Courtesy of Mamie Baldinger.)

GERMAN SIXTEEN CHURCH. Named for its location (16th Section of Tully Township) the German congregation of the church eliminated German references following the entry of the United States into World War I. (Courtesy of the Marion County Historical Society.)

MARTEL TILE COMPANY, ABOUT 1909. Before the advent of plastics, clay pottery fulfilled numerous duties around the house and in the field. "Tile" was needed to help drain farm fields of excess water. Glazed brick could be used for building sanitary structures such as dairies, and household earthenware was used to hold liquids, prepare meals, and store food. (Courtesy of the Marion County Historical Society.)

HAY. Hay comes from a variety of grasses (timothy and rye grass) and legumes (alfalfa and clover) grown throughout the planting season, to use for feed or in projects like building or drainage control. These Tully Township farmers are stacking hay—although the height of the stacks is exceptional. (Courtesy of the Marion County Historical Society.)

TULLY TOWNSHIP SCHOOL. During the "Good Schools" movement between 1910 and 1920, Tully Township officials built this school in Martel for their student body. It is interesting to note that the school system still depended on horse-drawn school wagons to get the students to the new building. (Courtesy of the Marion County Historical Society.)

MARTEL GIRLS' BASKETBALL. The 1936–1937 Martel Girls' Basketball Team posed in their uniforms for this image taken at the beginning of the season. Despite their best efforts, the team closed out the season with a 1-6 record; they did, however, top Agosta, which finished its season with a 0-5 record. (Courtesy of the Marion County Historical Society.)

Four

GRAND, SALT ROCK, AND BIG ISLAND TOWNSHIPS

Located in northwestern Marion County, Grand Township is so named because it originally contained three fully surveyed townships and enough Virginia Military Land for a fourth. It was reduced in size by the creation of Montgomery and Bowling Green Township in Marion County; it also yielded land for Marseilles and Mifflin Townships in Wyandot County. Grand is now the smallest township in the county. Its placement on the Sandusky Plains provides it with fertile soil and numerous freshwater springs. Aside from agriculture, the only other industry was quarrying. By 1826, a schoolhouse was found in Section 24, and the first church services were also held there.

Like Grand Township, Salt Rock Township is located partially on the Sandusky Plains. The township was reorganized in March 1845 to its present boundaries when it lost two tiers of sections on the north to Wyandot County. Ebenezer Roseberry came to the area in 1812 as a squatter. He told a story of stumbling over a white rock while chasing a wounded deer. It was so white that it looked like salt; so he broke off a piece and the township became "Salt Rock." In pioneer days, Native Americans visited this township more often than any other part of Marion County. The largest community in Salt Rock Township is the community of Morral.

Big Island Township is located south of Salt Rock Township. The "island" in the name of this township refers to a large grove of trees that the original settlers found in the midst of the prairie. The township was erected on March 5, 1823, from Salt Rock Township, its boundaries being unchanged since that date. By 1831, the crossroad at Big Island was a thriving community with three stores, two taverns, and a hotel in a brick building. The community was served by blacksmiths, wagon makers, shoemakers, coopers, carpenters, tailors, and three physicians. Now the Big Island Wildlife Area of the Ohio Department of Natural Resources preserves the marshes that foster waterfowl and wildlife.

RES. AND FARM VIEW OF **CHARLES BLOW ESQ.**

CHARLES BLOW FARM, GRAND TOWNSHIP. In 1878, the firm of Harrison, Sutton, and Hare published the *Atlas of Marion County Ohio*, an illustrated map of the county and the townships. In addition to mapping the roads through the county, the atlas also plotted the land ownership. Local residents, like Charles Blow, had the opportunity to buy space for illustrations of their property to include in the atlas. Itinerant artists traveled to the locations to be illustrated and made drawings for the engravers in Philadelphia to follow. Illustrations showed sylvan scenes of placid farms and the harmony between nature and agriculture. Family members of the patrons were often drawn into the images. Plump hogs, contented cattle, woolly sheep, and pastures of prancing horses spoke of the fine specimens to be found on each farm illustrated. (Courtesy of the Marion County Historical Society.)

DANIEL CLIFTON AND FAMILY. Daniel Clifton and his family posed for the image in front of their modest home near Espyville in Big Island Township in 1900. The photograph captures the reality of how many families of workers lived simply and without great flourishes. Clifton and his wife, Emma, pose with their children, Frank, Lizzie, Pearl, Ethel, and Gertrude. (Courtesy of Diana Hamm.)

FOR JESUS. Church members pose for their picture in front of the church in Espyville around 1900. In addition to providing a communal place of worship, rural churches also provided families with weekly social opportunities away from the solitude of farm life. (Courtesy of Diana Hamm.)

DECLIFF. This view of Decliff was taken from the church tower, looking toward the rail line and elevator. (Courtesy of the Marion County Historical Society.)

GREEN MILLER. Green Miller was a well-known Decliff store owner, carrying a general line of merchandise. Miller was murdered 1931 by transients who had come to Decliff after robbing another merchant in Kenton earlier the same day. (Courtesy of the Marion County Historical Society.)

MORRAL CANNING COMPANY, AROUND 1915. Before the advent of national brand canned goods, the local companies fulfilled the need to keep local stores stocked. The Morral Canning Company, erected in 1899, was one such business. If corn was in season, then corn was canned; the same went for peas, beans, and other items. Commercially canned foods were a luxury for many people, who saved money by canning their own garden vegetables and meat on the stoves in their homes. (Courtesy of the Marion County Historical Society.)

MORRAL SCHOOL, AROUND 1910. This building, built before Morral was incorporated as a village in 1904, was originally built to serve the "Morral Special School District." The building was doubled in size (the vertical seam down the middle of the facade is evident in this image) when the student population merited its enlargement. (Courtesy Craig Barnhart, Gary Barnhart collection.)

MORRAL SCHOOL. In 1916, Morral residents opened this modern facility, an outcome of the "Good Schools" movement sweeping Ohio. Just as in Caledonia, Kirkpatrick, Waldo, New Bloomington, Meeker, and Grand Prairie Township, advances in educational needs drove the push toward well-built modern buildings. Each of these schools were equipped with indoor sanitary plumbing, central heat, and electricity at a time when many rural homes had none of these features. Instead of all grades sharing one room, several grades shared a room, allowing for modern teaching methods. A gymnasium was added to the Morral building in 1938. Scott Township (later renamed Kirkpatrick) was the first of the northern systems to consolidate in 1948, when its students could choose between Claridon and Grand Prairie schools. Morral, Meeker, and Grand Prairie consolidated their systems in the 1950s to become Ridgedale Local Schools. The year 1957 marked the last graduating class from Morral, after which the school would be assigned to lower grades. Morral School was decommissioned in 2004 having served its students and community for 88 years. (Courtesy of Bill Schertzer.)

MORRAL BROTHERS MACHINE SHOP. Employees of the Morral Brothers Machine Shop pose for their picture with S. E. Morral (seated, center), foreman and owner of the company in 1937. The rest pictured are, from left to right, (first row) Thomas McCumber, Phillip Hartman, Fred Russell, Daniel Collins, Albert Carpenter, and Carl Moser; (second row) Albin Ferguson, Robert Schertzer, and Samuel Beck. (Courtesy of Stephanie Schertzer.)

SAY CHEESE. Jim Weston, Ray Weston, and Bob Cook enjoy a summer's moment aboard a John Deere tractor, parked on the Cook family's farm on Holland Road. Note that this tractor, built after World War II, was equipped with rubber tires instead of the steel wheel and blades used on older models. (Courtesy of Bob Cook.)

49

YFA BASKETBALL TEAM. Members of the Morral Young Farmers of America (YFA) basketball team pose for their photograph at the end of the 1940–1941 season. The team was of league basketball play and earned the championship that year. Seen here are, from left to right, (first row) Frank Minor, Ralph Beam, Donald Williams, Pinny Branch, and Donald Stein; (second row) Mr. Furnass (the high school coach), ? McWherter, Tug McWherter, Lloyd Cochran, Kensal Clutter, Sam Roberts, unidentified, Junior Bosley, and Mr. Bishop, YFA teacher. (Courtesy of Kensal Clutter.)

Five

MARION AND
MARION TOWNSHIP

Shortly before the War of 1812, a surveying party camped near the corner of what is now Delaware and Gurley Avenues. They found water but no settlers. Named Jacob's Well, this place became a stopping place for troops and supplies headed to Lake Erie. Alexander Berry purchased the site and settled it in 1820.

Eber Baker and Alexander Holmes filed the plat for the village of Marion on April 3, 1822, and it was named for the county that had been erected and named Marion by the Ohio legislature on February 20, 1820. When incorporated as a town in 1830, the first public building was on the northwest corner of the original plat and was used as a courthouse, school, and meetinghouse.

As the city of Marion grew and expanded its boundaries, acres of prime farmland yielded to the needs of the community. While there are subdivisions within Marion Township, a significant percentage of land remains under cultivation, especially north and west of the city of Marion.

Warren G. Harding, the 29th president of the United States, taught in the Marion Township School that was once located on the site presently occupied by radio station WMRN. Finding that teaching was not to his liking, he bought the struggling *Marion Star* newspaper and the rest is history.

BIRD'S-EYE VIEW OF MARION. This 1909 image of downtown Marion was taken standing atop the Huber Building elevator tower using several exposures that were then knitted together. When published by Wiant's, the image appeared on a 10-inch-long postcard. The most easily identified landmark is the Marion County Courthouse in the center of the image. But the image is also interesting because it shows other landmarks that are no longer standing. To the lower left center is a commercial building with the name "Stoltz" on it. The front of that structure was

once part of the old Presbyterian church in Marion. Sweeping to the right side of the image, beyond the Bennett Block's tower, is a square building in the distance that once housed the Central Emergency Hospital. Further to the right in the far distance is the old water company standpipe, a water tower of sorts that helped to maintain water pressure for the system. And finally in the lower right corner is the tower of the Busby Block, which was razed in 2005 for Busby Park. (Courtesy of Craig Barnhart, Gary Barnhart collection.)

BURNS'S STORE AND THE GRIMM BLOCK, ABOUT 1870. A very early view of Robert Burns's store and the Grimm Block shows how busy South Main Street was in the years following the Civil War. Robert Burns is standing in the front doorway. To the right is a sign advertising "Coal Oil" for sale. (Courtesy of the Marion County Historical Society.)

CORNER OF MAIN AND CENTER STREETS. This rare night image, taken by Edward B. Vail, a noted Marion photographer, records the snowy intersection of Main and Center Streets at 10:00 p.m. on March 2, 1906. (Courtesy of the Marion County Historical Society.)

HUGGINS-MUNSELL RESIDENCE, 1900. The Huggins-Munsell residence once stood at the southwest corner of Delaware Avenue and Washington Street. Sold in the late 1950s for development, the house was moved to Newmans-Cardington Road in Pleasant Township. CVS now occupies this site. (Courtesy of the Marion County Historical Society.)

WILSON RESIDENCE, 1890S. Members of the Wilson family pose in front of their home on the northeast corner of Center and Greenwood Streets. The family operated the S. Wilson and Son Nursery from their six-acre property. The endeavor holds the distinction of being the first grower in Marion to raise hybridized tomatoes. In the 1930s, a service station was built in the front yard of the home, and the address was moved to Greenwood Street. (Courtesy of Stephanie Schertzer.)

EMMANUEL HAMILTON FARMSTEAD, ABOUT 1910. This was the home of Emmanuel and Hattie (Search) Hamilton, on Route 4 north of Marion. The Hamiltons were the grandparents of Oliver and Merle Hamilton. When the house was razed by Oliver to build his house, the family was reminded that under the clapboard siding was a cabin dating from the earliest days of Marion County. (Courtesy of Oliver Hamilton.)

EMSINGER RESIDENCE. Located in northern Marion Township on Marion Williamsport Road is the Emsinger residence. Built in the 1880s, the house was enlarged through the extensive use of decorative stonework. (Courtesy of the Marion County Historical Society.)

KENYON MOORE RESIDENCE, AROUND 1900. Built in western Marion Township on the Green Camp Pike, now Bellfontaine Avenue, is the Kenyon Moore residence. The house is best remembered as the longtime residence of Mr. and Mrs. Walter D. Moore. (Courtesy of the Marion County Historical Society.)

MARION GRAIN AND SUPPLY, AROUND 1900. Established by Simon DeWolfe, this image of the Marion Grain and Supply Company was taken around 1900. The company served farmers and eventually city residents alike. (Courtesy of the Marion County Historical Society.)

CHILDREN NEAR THE ERIE YARDS, 1893. This image was taken by Chester L. Carlyle, a Marion High School student and amateur photographer. The image is important in that Carlyle's image shows the children as they were that day, and not in any type of contrived pose that played to stereotypes popular in the era. (Courtesy of Randy Winland.)

JUMP. Another image by Carlisle shows children being children, and playing around things that they ought not to have been playing around. In the photograph album where this and the image above were both mounted, Carlyle noted that the picture was taken with a shutter speed of 1/625 of a second. (Courtesy of Randy Winland.)

RICHLAND PIKE, 1900. This image from 1900 shows the Richland Pike, looking south toward the Dan Kaufman farmstead. Richland Pike took travelers south on a direct line to Richland Township until the 1960s. When U.S. Route 23 bypassed Marion, the road diverted to Somerlot-Hoffman Road for the trip over the divided highway below. (Courtesy of Helen Kauffman and Dorothy Young.)

DAN KAUFFMAN WITH DAISY AND DOLLY. Kauffman poses with his workhorses Daisy and Dolly in this pre–World War I image. Workhorses such as these were among the most important animals on a working farm and were used for pulling plows and wagons. (Courtesy of Helen Kauffman and Dorothy Young.)

HARDING MEMORIAL DEDICATION, JUNE 16, 1931. Though the bodies of Pres. Warren G. Harding and former first lady Florence Kling Harding were entombed at the finished Harding Memorial in 1927, the monument to the nation's 29th president was not dedicated until 1931. Political scandals involving Harry Daugherty, Albert Fall, and Charles Forbes, along with the legally unproven claims of Nan Britton and Gaston Means (a con man and later convicted murderer) cast a dim light on Harding in popular culture. Harding's accomplishments of lower taxes, creation of the Bureau of Veterans Affairs, establishment of the Office of the Budget, and the call to end discrimination and lynching of African Americans in the United States were, and continue to be, overlooked and forgotten. After Ohio officials and the press began to apply pressure by calling attention to the "national shame" of the undedicated tomb, the ceremony was scheduled for June 1931. Pres. Herbert Hoover and his predecessor Calvin Coolidge attended the ceremony, which was also attended by a crowd estimated at approximately 50,000 people. President Hoover complained about the airplanes flying over the event—ironically one that took this image. (Courtesy of Stuart J. Koblentz.)

ANYTHING IS POSSIBLE. When Zenabelle Moehn decided that the walk from her family's home to Harding High School was too far, she went to work and earned enough teaching piano to buy this 1940 Indian motorcycle. This made Moehn the only Harding student who rode a motorcycle to school. (Courtesy of Zenabelle Messenger.)

A MARION TRADITION. Ice-cream places come and go, but Marion's Jer-Zee is an enduring tradition for more than 50 years. Opening advertisements guaranteed that there was "a curl on every cone." The Jer-Zee is located at the corner of Center Street and Forest Lawn Boulevard and is currently owned by Dean and Barb Pine. (Courtesy of Stuart J. Koblentz.)

MARION PLAZA. Marion's first planned suburban-style shopping center was the Marion Plaza in eastern Marion Township. This picture was taken in the fall of 1959, when the Big Bear Grocery Store was being readied to open. The plaza also housed a Kroger's, Plaza Lanes, Woolworth's Five and Dime Store, and specialty shops. The center also contained one department store, Miller's. Welles Discount Department Store also opened in Marion Plaza after completing its own building on the site. (Courtesy of Stuart J. Koblentz.)

LK SOUTH. Founded in Marion by Cleo Ludwig and Robert Kibby, LK Restaurants were a longtime mainstay in Marion and the Midwest. The original LK Restaurant was located on West Center Street at Olney Avenue. The LK Restaurant South was one of the first local businesses to expand to the Delaware Avenue corridor following the Korean War. The site is now occupied by Mathew's Acura. (Courtesy of the Marion County Historical Society.)

HY-WAY ROLLERENA. The Hy-Way Rollerana was located on East Center Street at Parkview Avenue. Following the closure of Crystal Lake's Roller Rink, the Hy-Way Rollerena was the place to skate in Marion. (Courtesy of Craig Barnhart, Gary Barnhart collection.)

ROLLERENA. The skating rink's management used images of the "rollerena" in its advertising to convey grace and beauty. (Courtesy of Rhea Poulster.)

HY-WAY
ROLLARENA
MARION, OHIO

BURRIS AND EDWARDS, ARCHITECTS. Perhaps no other architectural firm in Marion represented cutting edge design more than Burris and Edwards. The firm's office, located on Fairfax Road, complimented the Marion County Bank South branch (now Chase Bank). Now Burris and Behne, the firm continues to innovate through its designs. This image, used on one of the firm's Christmas cards in the 1960s, provides a stunning view of the offices at night. (Courtesy of Marion County Historical Society.)

U.S. Route 23. Completed in the late 1960s, U.S. Route 23 cut a wide swath through Marion County and removed traffic congestion from downtown. The highway also shifted development and many retail jobs toward the eastern half of Marion County. (Courtesy of the Marion County Historical Society.)

Marion-Mount Gilead Road, Looking East, 1970. This image was taken in the summer of 1970 when the Ohio Department of Transportation began the process of widening Marion-Mount Gilead Road from a two-lane country road to a five-lane highway from the city limits to the US 23 bypass east of Marion. The grove of trees beyond the shopping center marked the beginning of the Marion County Home property. (Courtesy of the Marion County Engineers Office.)

Epworth Methodist Church Kindergarten, around 1954. Prior to school-established kindergartens, families in Marion County optionally enrolled their children in classes operated by local churches and organizations. This class from Epworth Methodist Church was on a tour of Isaly's Dairy on East Center Street. (Courtesy of Babette Dusang-Jones.)

Frontier Days, 1954. Employees of the S. S. Kresge's Store in downtown Marion pose in costume during Marion's annual Frontier Days sale. All the downtown merchants joined in the fun of the sale that was held each fall. (Courtesy of Stuart J. Koblentz.)

JUNIOR LECTURE RECITAL CLUB, 1954. Members of Marion's Junior Lecture-Recital Study Club pose for their picture in the ballroom of the Harding Hotel. Club programs included both musical and oratory presentations. Members in this picture are, from left to right, (first row) Jane Haley, Evelyn Price, Jeanne Bibbe, Helen Berg, Mary Kay Mills, Sally Schneider, Carolyn Jones, Joan Neidhart, and Roger Jamison; (second row) Linnea Gonzalez, Rosemary Sidenstricker, Kay Montgomery, Carol Sue Keck, Susan Kinsler, Madelyn Marsh, Nancy Hammond, David Richards, Gary Parish, and Ben Bechtel. (Courtesy of Stuart J. Koblentz.)

GOLD STAR MOTHERS. The Marion chapter of the Gold Star Mothers posed for this 1953 image. Membership in the organization was limited to the mothers of United States servicemen and servicewomen who sacrificed their lives for their country while in the U.S. Army, Navy, Marines, or Coast Guard. (Courtesy of Stuart J. Koblentz.)

MARION COMMUNITY ORCHESTRA. Without an organized professional orchestra of its own, members of the Marion County musical community joined together in the 1950s to form the Marion Community Orchestra. This picture, taken by Carl Stewart, was taken in the mid-1960s to publicize a coming concert. (Courtesy of Stuart J. Koblentz.)

THE FOLLIES. From the 1950s through the 1980s, one of the biannual highlights for Marionites was the Junior Service Guild's (JSG) Follies. The JSG Follies were community-wide productions, featuring top directors and scripts combined with lavish scenery and musical numbers. This promotional image was taken in the early 1960s and features, from left to right, Marilyn Babich, Bertha Altmaier, and Martha Moore. (Courtesy of Stuart J. Koblentz.)

Six

MONTGOMERY, BOWLING GREEN, AND GREEN CAMP TOWNSHIPS

Montgomery Township was set off from Grand Township—once the largest township in Marion County—in December 1831. Daniel Markley came about 1820, and Col. William Cochran acquired 80 acres in 1823. A post office was established in his house, and the village became known as Cochranton. The name was later changed to Meeker. In 1825, Maj. William LaRue established LaRue Village, whose citizens built the first bridge across the Scioto in 1843. The community of Carey Station was laid out in 1856 by W. W. and Wingate Carey. The name changed to New Bloomington about 1879 and to Agosta on April 1, 1883. After World War II, Agosta again became New Bloomington.

Bowling Green Township, originally part of the Virginia Military district, was named by Thomas Parr for the township in Licking County where he previously dwelt. It was originally included in Grand and Montgomery Townships before being erected Bowling Green Township on March 5, 1838. In 1824, a tornado cleared timber in a strip nearly a mile wide in the area and was known as "Windfall." In 1828, a fire burned trees, brush, and weeds, clearing the ground for cultivation. A hand-drawn map in the Marion County Engineers office illustrates the "windfall" and the "burn," showing the degree of damage from east to west. In the spring of 1829, this cleared land attracted settlers including Parr, who laid out Holmesville. At one time Holmesville had a post office, tavern, dry goods store, two groceries, a blacksmith, and a wagon shop. Nothing remains of that community today.

Green Camp Township, drained by the Scioto River and tributaries, is where the Little Scioto River joins the Scioto River. A blockhouse was erected here during the War of 1812, and Captain Green camped here, for which the township was named. It reached its present boundaries in 1838. In 1843, John Bradshaw moved into a house on the site of the present Methodist church and operated the Halderman-Fisk Mill. The village of Berwick was laid out in June 1838 by David Beach. Upon incorporation in 1875, the name changed to Green Camp. In the 1880s, second-generation German families moved into the township. The Green Camp Prairie, one of two protected prairie remnants in Marion County, is owned by the Marion County Historical Society and is rich in native grasses and other indigenous plant specimens.

GUTHERY CATTLE DRIVE THROUGH LaRUE, PRE–WORLD WAR I. In the era before trucking livestock became the rule of the day, if a breeder or farmer wanted to receive animals from a shipper or send animals to buyer, the only way to get the animals from the farm to the freight train was overland by driving the cattle to the destination. This image was taken at the intersection of what is now State Routes 95 and 37 in LaRue. (Courtesy of Jim Anderson.)

LaRue Ohio. While this image of LaRue from 1915 may make it look like a sleepy village, there was a lot to do in this western Marion County community. As the largest village in western Marion County, LaRue contained markets, churches, schools, and professional services. (Courtesy of Randy Winland.)

Sawyer's Sanitarium
LA RUE - OHIO.

TERMS
FURNISHED ON
APPLICATION.

Dr. Sawyer's LaRue Sanatorium. Before opening his state-of-the-art sanatorium in Marion, Dr. Charles E. Sawyer operated this three-building medical compound in LaRue in 1891. Sawyer closed this operation in 1892, moved briefly to Indianapolis for training, and then returned to Marion in 1893. (Courtesy of Stuart J. Koblentz.)

LaRue School. Built in 1890, this structure served as LaRue's school building until it was destroyed by fire on February 2, 1907. The exterior design was one of the most highly ornamented Richardson Romanesque–styled buildings in Marion County, second only to that of Marion's 1894 high school structure that formerly stood on West Center Street. (Courtesy of Randy Winland.)

LaRue Farmers Exchange, about 1910. Goods, animals, and crops produced by farmers and livestock breeders could be sold at the LaRue Farmer's Exchange. In this image, the men are posed with bags of seed corn. (Courtesy of the Marion County Historical Society.)

SCHMIDT FAMILY PREPARES FOR ARIZONA. Fred and Ruth Schmidt and their children, Don and Doris (along with an unidentified man), pose by the Schmidts' automobile prior to driving to Arizona in the early spring of 1925. Fred had tuberculosis, and the family hoped that the dry Arizona air would ease his condition. The family returned to Ohio shortly after arriving in Arizona, finding the circumstances unsatisfactory. Tuberculosis was commonly found in the population until the 1950s. Carriers of the disease could be infected for years before showing symptoms and often infected other members of their families. The treatment for the potentially lethal disease ranged from fresh-air cures and rest to radical surgery techniques. Some procedures included crushing the nerve that controls the cough reflex, forced compression (rest) of the lung through gas injection into the lining of the lung, or lung removal. The disease, however, was most dangerous when it would spread from the patients' lungs to their kidneys, liver, heart, pancreas, or brain. If left untreated, the prognosis of death was almost certain. (Courtesy of Opal Clutter.)

ST. JOSEPH'S CATHOLIC CHURCH. LaRue was unique in rural Marion County's religious landscape in that it was home to St. Joseph's Catholic Church, the only ongoing parish outside of the city of Marion. One of the oldest churches in LaRue, the church celebrated its final mass in 2006. (Courtesy of Jim Anderson.)

PROPOSED ELGIN HIGH SCHOOL. As part of the 1950s consolidation of village and township schools, Montgomery, Bowling Green, and Green Camp Townships, along with New Bloomington School and LaRue, joined together to form the Elgin School District. Prospect also joined the district before the high school was dedicated in November 1962. (Courtesy of Randy and Sandy Winland.)

W. P. LaRue Farm, 1907. Named for his uncle, LaRue founder Maj. William LaRue, William P. LaRue purchased and operated this farm of 190 acres two and half miles northeast of LaRue, beginning in 1901. The child in the image is the LaRues' youngest daughter, Flora. (Courtesy of the Marion County Historical Society.)

NEW BLOOMINGTON SCHOOL BAND. Members of the New Bloomington School Band pose for their picture in this image from 1946. Included in their schedule was "Santa and His Toyland Review" performed in December of that year. (Courtesy of Martha Harruff Chapman.)

ATOMIC BLONDE. The junior class play for New Bloomington School in 1955 was the *Atomic Blonde*. The cast of the play included, from left to right, (first row) Martha Harruff, Linda Harrison, Jackie Brinkley, John Gracely, Martha Ann Kalb, Carole Sharp, Earl Lee Harrison, Barbara Prettyman, Janet Tron, Don Van Wey, and Richard Lyon; (second row) Carl Breece, Erdis Carr, Richard Shirea, and Floyd Beers. (Courtesy of Martha Harruff Chapman.)

BOWLING GREEN SUBORDINATE GRANGE. Members of the Bowling Green Township Subordinate Grange pose for their group picture in 1938. Subordinate (local) Granges were community-based organizations, open to men, women, and teenagers of ages 14 and up. All members were accepted with full membership rights and conferred the first of four ritualistic degrees. (Courtesy of the Marion County Historical Society.)

BOWLING GREEN GRANGE DRILL TEAM, AROUND THE 1930S. As part of its community-based programming, the Bowing Green Grange organized a drill team. Members included, from left to right, (first row) Ruth Denman, Evelyn Shuster, Mary Grappy, Dorothy Jean Wilson, Faye Flesher, Della Cochran, Anna Mae Grappy, Cecilia Snyder, and Gladys Rosebrough; (second row) Grace Clunk, Preston Owen, Kenny Ruth, Clay Tilton, Eston Williams, Ralph Amstutz, Ervin Ricketts, Cletus Snyder, and Don Oberdier. (Courtesy of the Marion County Historical Society.)

GREEN CAMP, ABOUT 1900. Not on the regular Columbus, Delaware, and Marion (CD&M) interurban route, Green Camp did, for a time, enjoy traction services when a spur was built that connected the community to the main CD&M line. Note the unimproved (and muddy) street—a messy reminder of how residents lived before the advent of paved streets. (Courtesy of Mike and Linda Perry.)

BUCKEYE STEAM DITCHER, ABOUT 1910. The best fields for farming are well drained, either naturally, or by laying drainage tile. This early, steam-powered ditching machine, with a 10-foot digging wheel, was a technical advancement over hand digging ditches for tile. (Courtesy of Opal Clutter.)

78

RAILROAD BRIDGE, LITTLE SCIOTO RIVER, 1893. This picture of the railroad bridge over the Little Scioto River was taken by Marionite Chester L. Carlyle, an amateur photographer of great skill. Carlyle, an 1894 Marion High School graduate, went onto earn his medical degree from Western Reserve Medical College. Other images by Carlyle appear on page 58. (Courtesy of Randy Winland.)

TESTING THE WATERS, 1913. This engine ventured out over the tracks engulfed in floodwaters along the Little Scioto River, east of Green Camp. Flooding on the river was frequent in the late winter and early spring, but the flood of 1913 was a statewide disaster. If the engineer lost his nerve, the engine would be put into reverse and backed up to Green Camp until conditions improved. (Courtesy of Kensel Clutter.)

WILL ULLMER AND HIS SLEIGH, AROUND 1915. Will Ullmer and his sleigh pose in front of the family residence on Ground Hog Pike. Sleighs were not just for joyrides before the introduction of improved roads. If the roads were snow packed (or ice coated), sleighs were the most efficient way to get about. The community members would also have to make sure that bridges were coated in snow to allow the sleighs to cross the bridge without grinding the runners on the bridge decks. (Courtesy of Nancy Gracely.)

GOODRICH PLANT, 1951. In January 25, 1951, tire manufacturer BF Goodrich broke ground for a Marion County facility outside of Green Camp. The facility, built by the locally owned General Contracting Company, was opened in 1951 and produced high-compression hose lines. (Courtesy of the Marion County Historical Society.)

Seven

JIM THORPE, THE OORANG YEARS

Jim Thorpe is widely recognized as the all-around top American athlete of the 20th century. Born Jacobus Franciscus Thorpe, to an Irish American father and a Sac and Fox mother, his native name was Wa-Tho-Huk. Thorpe showed his athletic prowess at an early age. Thorpe was a member of the 1912 United States Olympic Team and won the gold medal in the pentathlon and decathlon. King Gustav V of Sweden declared Thorpe to be "the greatest athlete in world." Thorpe's gold medals were revoked in 1913 when it was discovered that he had received money for playing professional baseball. After losing the medals, Thorpe received offers to play professional baseball, but football was his competitive sport of choice.

After playing for the Canton Bulldogs football team, Thorpe was introduced to Walter Lingo of LaRue. Lingo was impressed with Thorpe and decided to apply for a National Football League (NFL) franchise of his own. Lingo's plan was to use the team as advertising for his Oorang Kennels in LaRue. Thus LaRue became the smallest community ever awarded an NFL team. Lingo's Oorang Indians team was comprised entirely of Native Americans who not only played for the team, but also performed in costume during each halftime held for the games they played. Lingo is credited with inventing the tradition of half-time entertainment. When the team was not playing football, they lived in LaRue and worked for Lingo, tending the dog kennels. The team only played during the 1922 and 1923 football seasons before Lingo decided to exit football to focus on other methods of promoting his kennels and King Oorang breed of Airedale terriers. Thorpe and Lingo remained friends for many years.

While not widely known, Thorpe also played professional basketball on an all–Native American basketball team, the World Famous Indians. The topic of Thorpe playing basketball received national attention in 2006 when it was a topic on the PBS television program *History Detectives*.

The name Oorang is not of American origin. Lingo purchased a dog that was sired by a male dog named Oorang, allegedly after King Oorang of Sweden.

OORANG KENNELS ADVERTISEMENT. Walter Lingo was a promoter at heart. When he entered into the dog breeding business, he advertised the business in national periodicals, with colorful advertisements; sales rose sufficiently to make the endeavor a profitable business. (Courtesy of Jim Anderson.)

WALTER LINGO AND JIM THORPE. Lingo and Jim Thorpe (center and right) pose with an unidentified man and several (Oorang-bred) hounds in this promotional picture dating from about 1922. (Courtesy of Jim Anderson.)

COONPAW INN. When living in LaRue, Thorpe and his family lived for a time at the Coonpaw Inn, named for its owner. The inn also housed several other players on the team. The structure was lost to fire in the 1990s. (Courtesy of Jim Anderson.)

JIM THORPE IN UNIFORM. Thorpe poses in his Oorang Indians football uniform. Players in the 1920s relied heavily on leather-made articles to perform the job of protecting the players from injury. The team's logo was the letter *I* placed over top of an O. (Courtesy of Jim Anderson.)

NFL OORANG INDIANS, 1922. Walter Lingo, far left, poses with members of the Oorang Indian football team. Jim Thorpe is standing in the center rear. In addition to playing football, the team also entertained the crowds during half-time shows promoting Lingo's Oorang Kennels. (Courtesy of Jim Anderson.)

OORANG PRACTICE, LARUE. Thorpe is identified in this image showing the team at practice in LaRue. While good athletes, the team's overall record in its two seasons of play were losing ones of 3-6 in 1922 and 1-10 in 1923. (Courtesy of Jim Anderson.)

JIM THORPE PLAYS BASKETBALL. While it is widely known that Thorpe played football and baseball professionally, his basketball years are less widely known. This image is one of the very few of Thorpe in uniform for the World Famous Indians basketball team. While many of the players lived in Marion County, the team was a traveling team, almost exclusively playing its games on the road. (Courtesy of Jim Anderson.)

Two
Famous
Sports

The World's Greatest All-round Sportsman and Athlete, Jim Thorpe, with the World's Greatest All-round Sporting and Utility Dog, Lion Oorang.

PROMOTING THE OORANG AIREDALE. Thorpe continued to help Lingo promote Oorang Airedales in advertisements placed in magazines and newspapers. Lingo's kennels suffered during the Depression, and despite efforts to reintroduce true Oorang-bred dogs, the enterprise closed. (Courtesy of Jim Anderson.)

85

GRACE THORPE AND JIM ANDERSON, 1997. Grace Thorpe, talking with Oorang Indians chronicler Jim Anderson, is the daughter of Jim Thorpe. Grace returned to LaRue in 1997 to join in the festivities celebrating her father and the team's presence in the western Marion County village. (Courtesy of Jim Anderson.)

GRACE THORPE READING THE UNVEILED MARKER. As part of the celebration of the Oorang Indians in 1997, Grace was given the honor of unveiling the State of Ohio Historical Marker (marker 7-51) honoring the team and her father. The marker was installed at 300 South High Street (State Route 37) in LaRue. (Courtesy of Jim Anderson.)

Eight

CLARIDON, PLEASANT, AND RICHLAND TOWNSHIPS

Claridon, at the crossroads of the Marion-Mount Gilead and Whetstone River Roads, was the first village platted within Marion County. It was recorded by James Kilbourne on August 25, 1821, and he proposed it for the county seat. Caledonia, originally named Van Buskirk, was surveyed, platted, and acknowledged on December 30, 1834. He opened a country store, as did William Farrington. Caledonia was home to the George T. Harding family at one time. The Hardings' son, Warren, worked for the local newspaper the *Caledonia Argus* and would say later in his life that his time spent at the *Argus* was where the "newspaper bug" first bit him.

Named for its pleasant rolling vistas, Pleasant Township was organized on June 8, 1824, at the first session of the Marion County commissioners. By 1845, its present boundaries were established. Jacob Idleman arrived in February 1820 and settled in the area known as "Slab Camp," occupied by Gen. William Henry Harrison's troops during the War of 1812. John and Susannah Jones arrived from Pennsylvania with their large family that spring, offering their home as one of the first schools in the community and as the first Presbyterian house of worship. Later the strong tide of German families formed several "kolonies" (colonies) including the one along Bethlehem Road and the Zion kolonie to the northeast. German was the language of the home, school, and church, and the population of the township grew from 426 in 1830 to 1,414 in 1840. During the school consolidation in the 1950s, Pleasant Township opted to remain independent and remains so today.

Richland Township's rich, black prairie soil provided its name when organized by the Marion County Commissioners on June 8, 1824. The Greenville Treaty line marks its southern boundary. After 1830, the population grew from 414 to 1,138 in 1840 due to the arrival of German settlers including the Jacoby, Retterer, and Heinemann families. Henry Worline established the first sawmill in the county along the Whetstone River in 1821. S. W. Knapp ran a gristmill nearby from 1824 to 1844. In 1827, Titus King erected a fulling and carding mill. These mills provided early settlers with lumber, clothing, cornmeal, and flour. Joseph Morris, a Quaker, was an early nurseryman. His home on the northwest corner of State Routes 529 and 746 was a station on the Underground Railroad.

CLARIDON HOTEL. Travel in the mid-19th century was undertaken by necessity for most and for fun by those who had the time and money to commit to the journey. This structure once housed the Claridon Hotel, which provided guest rooms and meals for boarders. (Courtesy of Louise Haley.)

JAMES FOOS FARMSTEAD, AROUND 1898. James Foos and his wife, Rhoda Lindsey Foos, stand in front of their Claridon Township home. To the right of the couple is their son Will Foos, his wife, Maggie, and their daughter Lewella. (Courtesy of Kensel and Opal Clutter.)

RICE'S MILL, AROUND 1890. In 1880, Melvin Rice and E. M. Woodbridge purchased this sawmill in Caledonia and operated it together for a number of years. Rice and his family, along with their employees, posed for this image around 1890. (Courtesy of Diana Hamm.)

MYERS FAMILY REUNION. The children of Nelson and Isabel Miller Myers pose at the Myers home in Caledonia for this picture in 1909. The Myers children married into the Stafford, Osborne, Winters, Henry, Scott, Kennedy, and Rinehart families. Also in the group is Isabel's daughter by a previous marriage. (Courtesy of Stuart J. Koblentz.)

SILO CONSTRUCTION, WILLIAM SWAYZE AYE FARM. Silos perform the important job of crop storage on a working farm. The traditional method of building silos in the early 1900s was to use wood planks laid end to end in a circle and then bind the planks with iron rings to give support to the structure and to keep the silo walls from budging under the load stress of the silage. If a silo burned because of lightning or carelessness, the crops and the wooden planks were burnt to ash, leaving a pile of iron rings behind as a reminder of what was lost. (Courtesy of Scott Kelly.)

BRIDGE COLLAPSE, AROUND 1911. Early iron bridges were stronger than wooden bridges, but only to a point. This collapse occurred near the William Swayze Aye farm in the late winter of 1911. Ironically the engine bearing the wagons of crushed stone was in transit to shore up another bridge, in preparation for the moving of glacial erratic from the Aye farm to the Claridon Cemetery. (Courtesy of Don Underwood.)

90

MOVING THE ERRATIC, 1909. This 60-ton erratic, measuring 10 by 12 feet was moved from the William Swayze Aye farm two miles west to the Claridon Cemetery to mark the grave of William Swayze Aye. It was identified as a "Gowganda tillite," which is a metamorphic composite rock that originated near Lake Huron. It is called an "erratic" because it was pushed southward in an erratic fashion during the 18 ice shelf advances and retreats during the ice age. (Courtesy of Don Underwood.)

AN ERRATIC CROSSING OF THE WHETSTONE, 1909. Once underway, it was found that the bridge across the Whetstone River would not support the weight of the 80-ton erratic, so a temporary wooden bridge, mounted on tree stump pilings, was completed to move the boulder toward Claridon. The move was made by M. Mills and his employees for the sum of $1,500, without the aid of a steam shovel. (Courtesy of Don Underwood.)

CALEDONIA PUBLIC SCHOOL. Caledonia Public School, built in 1910, was an outgrowth of the Progressive Era and its school reforms. Structures like Caledonia provided students with modern facilities, equipped with electricity, sanitary plumbing, and central heat, while housing classes that would have normally spread throughout many one-room schoolhouses. (Courtesy of Randy Winland.)

HOLVERSTOTT'S MAPLE LEAF FARM. The Holverstott family was well known in Marion County for many years during the 19th and early-20th centuries. Maple Leaf Farm was located on Patton Pike and owned by the Holverstotts until purchased by the Earl family. (Courtesy of Nancy Earl.)

SECOND LIKENS CHAPEL. Located at the intersection of Likens and Pole Lane Roads, this building served as the Likens Methodist Episcopal Chapel from 1916 to 1942. Seized on May 1, 1942, for the Scioto Ordnance Plant, the church buildings escaped the wrecking ball when an engineer pled his case for the buildings' usability to the board overseeing the plant site. (Courtesy of the Marion County Historical Society.)

LIKENS CHAPEL CONGREGATION, APRIL 26, 1942. Members of Likens Chapel pose for their photograph on the final church service held in the building for the duration of the war. Many of the people pictured sacrificed land, their homes, and their livelihoods for the war effort. The congregation reformed following the war and then permanently merged with Kirkpatrick's congregation in the 1980s. (Courtesy of the Marion County Historical Society.)

THE HONEYMOON CABIN. One of the oldest structures razed during the Scioto Ordnance Plant takeover was the Seckle family's "Honeymoon" cabin, which dated from the 1820s. Though sided over, the cabin was built of logs and its joints daubed with the traditional clay and straw mixture. The brick chimney on the left side of the image emerged from the east wall at a height of five feet and was supported by two-by-fours. (Courtesy of Mr. and Mrs. Fred Haas.)

SCIOTO ORDNANCE PLANT BUILDING, AROUND 1950. The Scioto Ordnance Plant encompassed a 12,000-acre block of Marion County, taken by the federal government on May 1, 1942. The plant built fuses, shells, incendiary bombs, and napalm barrel bombs for the war effort. Following the war, farmers were offered the opportunity to repurchase their farms. The remaining buildings were converted to peacetime use. (Courtesy of the Marion County Historical Society.)

MEMORIAL METHODIST EPISCOPAL CHURCH. Caledonia Memorial Methodist Episcopal Church was a gift to the community by Standard Oil heiress Mrs. Steven B. Harkness, whose mother was a native of Caledonia. The structure was designed by noted Cleveland architect Charles Schweinfurth, who also designed Trinity Baptist Church in Marion. (Courtesy of Randy Winland.)

TREASURES AT THE FARM SALE. Trella Romine tries out a wooden wagon like the one she had as a child while attending the Roberts farm auction in 1990. Farm sales are a part of life in the country—a lifetime of treasures is sold to the highest bidders. (Courtesy of Trella Romine.)

TERRADISE. Given to the people of Marion County as a nature preserve, Terradise was built by Ray and Trella Romine in 1953. Overlooking the Whetstone River, the name Terradise comes from the words *terra* (for earth) and *dise* (from paradise). As a nature preserve, the natural beauty of Terradise is guaranteed for generations to come. (Courtesy of Trella Romine.)

COMER FAMILY, PLEASANT TOWNSHIP, AROUND 1910. Before the advent of inexpensive cameras, local photographers would travel the countryside and stop at farms to take pictures of families and their homes. If the men were in the field, they were called back in to have their pictures taken. In some cases folks cleaned up before being photographed, while others took it as a "come as you are" event. (Courtesy of Carol Robinson.)

JOHN SEITER CABIN, ABOUT 1930. This image was taken in the 1930s of the old John Seiter family cabin. After families graduated to modern houses, many cabins were used as tenant houses or machinery sheds. An advertising sign on the cabin promotes "Battle Axe" brand cleanser. (Courtesy of Craig Barnhart, Gary Barnhart collection.)

JOHN SEITER RESIDENCE. Located southeast of the Pleasant schools is the John Seiter residence, which was typical of a home befitting a successful farmer in the mid-1800s. Seiter cut the scrollwork for the residence's gables himself, according to a notation left by his daughter Matilda, because "father wanted to make sure it was done correctly." Note how the scrollwork allows shadows of its shapes to silhouette on the house. (Courtesy of Craig Barnhart, Gary Barnhart collection.)

CD&M INTERURBAN CAR, 1910. The Columbus, Delaware and Marion Traction Company (CD&M) interurban line provided residents of Marion the opportunity to travel between Marion, Delaware, and Columbus (plus the towns served in between) for a small sum in well-appointed electric cars that traveled up to 70 miles an hour. From Marion, the line traveled south along Route 4 toward Prospect, and from there toward Delaware. The line closed in 1932 due financial reasons made worse by the Great Depression. (Courtesy of the Marion County Historical Society.)

CD&M POWER STATION EMPLOYEES, 1937. The CD&M erected its electrical generating plant in southwestern Pleasant Township, along the Scioto River near Prospect. While interurban service ended in 1932, the CD&M power plant continued to generate electricity for Marion and southern Marion County into the 1960s. (Courtesy of the Marion County Historical Society.)

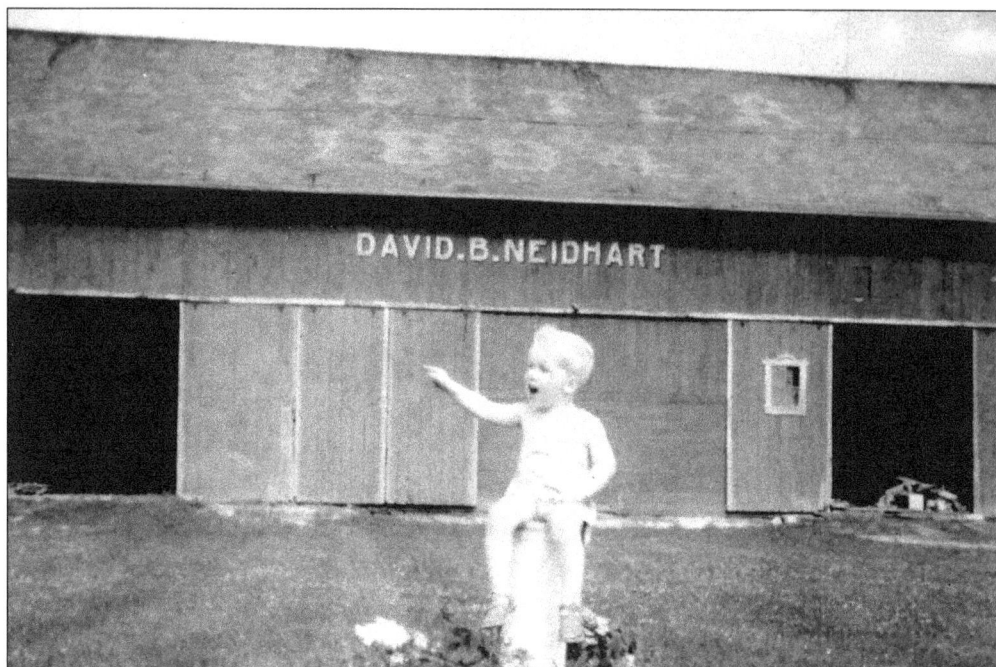

DAVID NEIDHART BARN. Mary Ellen Dune provided this 1953 image of her son David Neidhart perched atop a birdbath stand in front of his grandfather's barn in Pleasant Township. The barn, built in 1894 by Ed Neidhart's grandfather, burned to the ground one week later. (Courtesy of Mary Ellen Dune.)

ED NEIDHART BARN CONSTRUCTION. To replace the 1894 barn, Ed chose to go with a modern construction system. While the ground floor of the new barn was block, the rafters of the barn were prefabricated of laminated wood, allowing the upper stories to be free from obstructions. Moving hay to the mow was accomplished through a modern mechanical system. Like its predecessor, this barn was also lost in a fire in the 1980s. (Courtesy of Carroll Neidhart.)

EWE HAD A CLOSE SHAVE. Ed
Neidhart shears a sheep with
his sons Carroll (left) and David
looking on for the camera.
Shearing is one of the duties on
a working farm, making sheep
and their wool one of the more
renewable commodities on a farm.
(Courtesy of Mary Ellen Dune.)

MUSKRAT LOVE. Another image
provided by Mary Ellen Dune
is this image of her sons, David
(right), Carroll (center), and John,
proudly presenting a muskrat
to their parents: "One half for
Daddy and one half for Mommy."
(Courtesy of Mary Ellen Dune.)

Pleasant Local High School

PROPOSED PLEASANT LOCAL HIGH SCHOOL   A. H. MOELLERKAMP & ASSOCIATES

PROPOSED PLEASANT HIGH SCHOOL, MID-1950S. In order to keep pace with the post–World War II baby boom, Marion County schools began to consolidate the township school systems into better-funded regional districts. Plans had been proposed to unite Pleasant, Prospect, and Waldo Townships into a consolidated school system, however, Pleasant opted to remain independent; it was the only township system to do so. (Courtesy of Randy Winland.)

OWENS THEATRE. At the beginning of the 20th century, Owens Station was a thriving community. The limestone business was good, and the products were in demand. To provide entertainment for the residents, this theater was built and used for a number of years until the community started to break apart after the quarries closed. (Courtesy of Craig Barnhart, Gary Barnhart collection.)

CD&M Ohio Edison Scioto Plant. After being acquired by Ohio Edison, the CD&M electrical plant received a number of upgrades to keep it competitive in the electrical market. This composite image shows the plant and its staff in 1958 after its tall stack was completed. (Courtesy of the Marion County Historical Society.)

JOSEPH MORRIS HOUSE. Once located at the intersection of State Routes 529 and 746 in northeast Richland Township, this home, built by Joseph Morris, was a way station on the path to freedom for men and women escaping slavery in the southern United States. Accounts state that Morris, a Quaker, built the house with hidden compartments for the freedom seekers to hide in, and that a tunnel led to the barn and corn crib as well. (Courtesy of the Marion County Historical Society.)

OLDEST HOUSE IN MARION COUNTY, 1907. This house was identified as the oldest residence in continual use in Marion County in 1907. Carroll Neidhart believes that the house may have been built by the Jacoby family when they settled in Richland Township in the 1820s. Early settlers made do with what they had, but this house's continued use from pioneer days to the 1900s was a testament to its construction and usefulness. (Courtesy of Randy Winland.)

A WHETSTONE RIVER PICNIC, AROUND 1910. This group of revelers paused for a moment during an outing in 1910 to pose for a "brownie" snapshot of their afternoon. Even on such outings, it was then the fashion to be in fashion, even when relaxing on a summer's day in the country. (Courtesy of Carroll Neidhart.)

GIDDYUP, GOAT. This young man seems intent on taking his sled out for a spin in this winter scene in Richland Township. No word was recorded regarding the goat's performance, but chances are slim that the young one got the ride he was hoping to get. (Courtesy of Helen Kauffman.)

ON THE KRESS FARM. Members of the Kress family pose for the camera on their farm in Richland Township. Joining them are two members of their beef herd. (Courtesy of Helen Kauffman.)

Nine

PROSPECT AND WALDO TOWNSHIPS

It was not until June 1848 that today's Prospect Township had its present political boundaries, having been created from parts of Pleasant and Green Camp Townships and portions of Delaware County. However, since this was below the Greenville Treaty Line, the area had been settled on the west bank of the Scioto River by Darius and Cyre Landon by 1815. Originally called Middletown, in January 1876, upon petition of the citizens, the name was changed to Prospect since its "prospects" looked bright. The village of Prospect holds the title of largest incorporated village in Marion County, a position that it has held since the mid-1800s.

The land that now comprises Waldo Township was initially settled in February 1806 when members of the Wyatt and Brundage families came to the area. At that time the land located south of the Greenville Treaty line was part of Franklin County and known as Big Rock Township. A subsequent partition from Franklin County brought Big Rock Township under the governance of Delaware County. A village was laid out in 1831 by Milo D. Pettibone and named for his son Waldo. In 1848, the township was reassigned to Marion County and given the name Waldo Township. This was done as compensation to Marion County following the taking of three of Marion's eastern townships for the formation of Morrow County.

OLIVER NIEMEYER. Oliver Niemeyer was the principle photographer in Prospect in the early years of the 20th century. Although Niemeyer's works included studio portraits, he also is responsible for amassing a large collection of images in and around Prospect and throughout the community. (Courtesy of the Marion County Historical Society.)

NIEMEYER'S STUDIO, PROSPECT. Portrait studios in the 19th and early-20th century relied upon sunlight and when the sunlight was not sufficient, flash powder. Neimeyer's studio was equipped with a skylight and reflective surfaces used to control the lighting effects. (Courtesy of the Marion County Historical Society.)

RIZOR CABIN. The Rizor cabin was indicative of small cabins built by early settlers in southern Marion County. A cabin of this size would most likely contain a main room on the first floor and a loft or second floor. Such cabins were also built with one of their longest sides facing south, to get the most sun throughout the day. (Courtesy of the Marion County Historical Society.)

PAINE PETTIBONE LANDON. Paine Landon was among the first settlers to come to what is now Marion County, arriving with his parents around 1820 and settling on the west side of the Scioto River. According to notations made by his friend Ira C. Keller, Landon stated that "the woods were alive with deer, wolves, and Native Americans." (Courtesy of Ed Schweinfurth.)

PROSPECT ELEVATOR. Oliver Niemeyer captured this image of the Prospect Elevator undergoing foundation replacement. Shortly after the job was finished, the building was consumed by fire. (Courtesy of the Marion County Historical Society.)

UNION MILLS, ABOUT 1900. Union Mills stood for many years in the heart of Prospect. The company sold its milled wheat flour under the Starlight Flour and Starlight Corn Meal name brands. (Courtesy of the Marion County Historical Society.)

NATIONAL MILLS FIRE, 1908. In another image by Niemeyer, the fire that destroyed the National Mills in Prospect was recorded. According to the *Marion Star*, the fire was "especially hot considering the combustibility of the contents of the mill." (Courtesy of the Marion County Historical Society.)

BROOKSIDE FARM, AROUND 1900. Brookside Farm was the home of Ira Keller, a breeder of fine poultry. Keller promoted his Marion County poultry products as far as Madison Square Garden. Paine Pettibone Landon was a close friend of the family and kept in touch with the Kellers after relocating to Michigan. (Courtesy of Ed Schweinfurth.)

PROSPECT. Prospect is the largest village in Marion County, and this 1900s-era photograph shows the community's expansive footprint. But the image also shows the austere use of backyards in the early-20th century. At that time, backyards housed outhouses, barns, and vegetable gardens—some featured grape arbors. (Courtesy of the Marion County Historical Society.)

THE PLACID SCIOTO RIVER, PROSPECT. Under normal circumstances, the Scioto River at Prospect is a placid river, a place where one could boat in the summer and forget the cares of life. (Courtesy of Randy Winland.)

FLOODING AT PROSPECT, 1913. Residents of Prospect know that however placid the Scioto River can be, it can also bring damaging floods to their community. This image, looking west toward the bridge and the Watkins estate in the distance, illustrates the broad path that the river can cut when pushed by Mother Nature. (Courtesy of Carol Robinson.)

SULPHUR SPRINGS SANATORIUM, PROSPECT, AROUND 1900. Water cures became the rage in Europe during the early-19th century. These two young women visited the odorous sulphur springs of Dr. Samuel Gast's first sanatorium in Prospect. Regardless of its curative powers, sulphur water is an acquired taste and is best described as "water with some heft to it." (Courtesy of Randy Winland.)

SULPHOMAGNETIC SANATORIUM. Following a fire at the Gast sanatorium, a second, grander sanatorium was built. Joining the water cure was the application of "magneto" (electrical) treatments that were especially popular with women who found they relieved their stress. (Courtesy of the Marion County Historical Society.)

ED SCHWEINFURTH ON HIS CASE TRACTOR, AROUND 1940. Early tractors relied upon iron and steel wheels to cut through the dirt, mud, and muck and provided the needed traction to pull farm implements. This was accomplished with blades on the rear wheels. While effective in the field, these wheels were hard on paved surfaces and were replaced by rubber tires beginning in the 1930s. (Courtesy of Ed Schweinfurth.)

LIVING FLAG, 1940. Students at Prospect School demonstrate their patriotism by posing in this school tableau of the American flag. According to Opal Clutter, students were instructed to wear either red, white, or blue and then were directed as to where they would sit. (Courtesy of Opal Clutter.)

WALDO BRIDGE. For the first half of the 20th century, this iron truss bridge connected the village of Waldo to the east bank of the Whetstone River. After years of seasonal flooding, Waldo was separated from the river by the U.S. Army Corp of Engineers flood control program levy and later by the rerouting of U.S. Route 23 when it was rebuilt as a limited-access highway. (Courtesy of Randy Winland.)

STRAUB-ELLIOT HOUSE, WALDO. Built in the early 1800s by Andrew Straub, this building stood east of the Military Road (now Marion Street) connecting the territory south of the Greenville Treaty line with Fremont to the north. The structure, which was also the first post office in Waldo, was razed in the 1950s as the U.S. Army Corp of Engineers prepared the area for its flood control project that is now part of the Delaware Dam flood plain. (Courtesy of the Marion County Historical Society.)

JOHN STRINE RESIDENCE, AROUND THE 1930S. This house still stands on the east side of Marion Street in Waldo and was for many years the residence of the Strine family. (Courtesy of Mary Ellen Dune.)

OFFICE OF DR. B. D. OSBORN, WALDO. Dr. Osborn stands next to his early Ford Model T roadster, its canvas curtains in place for the winter. It was a chilly ride for those who would sit on the tonneau cover seat, a buckboard of sorts on the vehicle's rear deck. The building still stands, just south of the G&R Grille on Marion Street. (Courtesy of Randy Winland.)

WALDO TAVERN. A longtime landmark on Waldo's northern boundary was the Waldo Tavern, built in the 1840s to serve stagecoach riders along the Columbus-Sandusky Pike (now State Route 423). An effort to clean the building in the 1970s by sandblasting it resulted in damaging the face of the bricks, and the building's condition worsened. Ultimately the structure was razed despite ongoing efforts to preserve it. (Courtesy of Randy Winland.)

GRADING MARION STREET, WALDO. This image of a Marion steam shovel shows how the shovel was operated. The man to the front controlled the action of the machine, while the engineer monitored the firebox and water pressure needed to make the steam that drove the process of loading and unloading the bucket. (Courtesy of Randy Winland.)

Ten

SHOVEL CITY

For over 100 years, Marion was home to the leading producers and innovators of power shovels and draglines in the world. What was begun by Henry Barnhart and Edward Huber in 1884 would eventually lead Marion residents to produce 90 percent of all steam shovels in the world by 1910 through three major producers: Marion Steam Shovel, Fairbanks Steam Shovel, and the Osgood Shovel Company.

The first steam shovel in the world was built in 1835 in Philadelphia, based on the design patented by William Otis for the Garret and Eastwick Company. In 1883, Henry Barnhart approached Edward Huber with a design for a steam shovel, one that addressed the issues of weight, strength, and cost (which was an important issue in an era of cheap human labor). With Huber's financial backing, Barnhart built the first prototype, named Barnhart's Shovel and Wrecking Car. A patent was awarded to the pair in 1883, and along with George W. King, the Marion Steam Shovel Company (known locally as "the Shovel") was organized in August 1884. The company changed its name to Marion Power Shovel (MPS) in 1946 to more accurately address the product range and the advance of engine technology.

The Marion Shovel and Dredge Company (1910–1955) was founded by A. E. Cheney, who left Marion Steam Shovel after a disagreement with King. Cheney purchased the rights of the defunct Osgood Dredge Company of Albany, New York. Osgood Dredge Company had been established by William Carmichael, nephew of William Otis, the steam shovel's inventor. Osgood Dredge Company introduced the "steam shovel that works backwards" better known as dragline, in 1884. Cheney moved the company to Marion in 1910 and began production of smaller, more flexible shovel products. Though closed, Cheney, Otis, and Osgood Streets in southern Marion are a reminder of Osgood Shovel Company's days in Marion.

Marion's role in engineering and producing new shovels and draglines has ended, but the rich heritage that these machines and their manufacturers have left upon the community is immense, and so Marion rightfully holds the title of the "Shovel City."

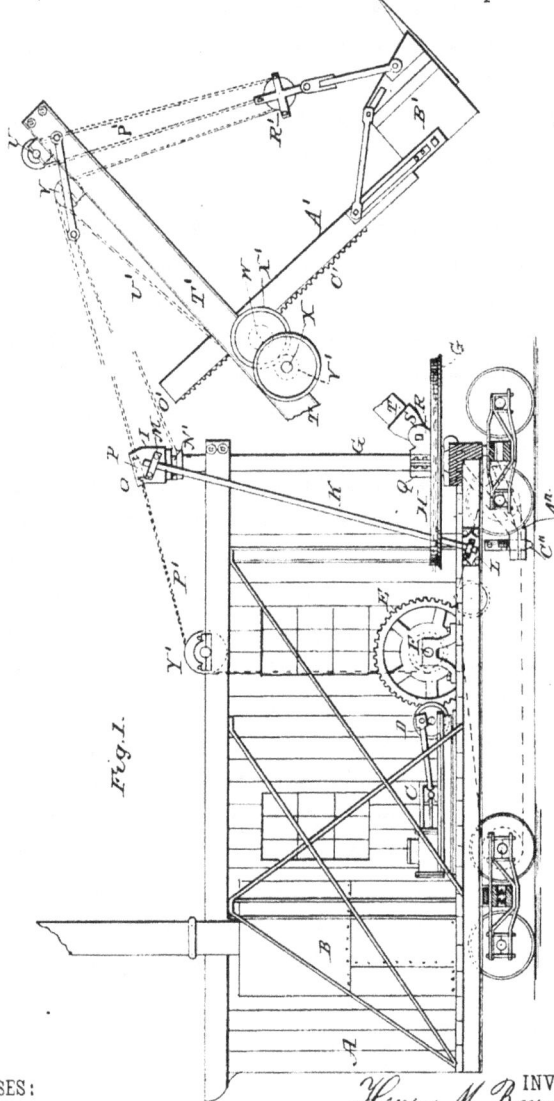

BARNHART'S DITCHER, AROUND THE LATE 1880S. This model, based on Barnhart's second shovel design, was mounted to a wooden barge that traveled forward in the ditch as it was dug. Massive wooden struts were adjusted through gears and acted to stabilize the machine and its housing as it moved forward. (Courtesy of the Marion County Historical Society.)

MARION SHOVEL MODEL NO. 36. Photographed while working on the South Prospect Street sewer project was this model No. 36 owned by the Evans Quarry in Marion. The 30 Series shovels were the first fully revolving shovels produced by the company. (Courtesy of the Marion County Historical Society.)

FAIRBANKS SHOVEL COMPANY, ABOUNT 1910. Marion was also the home of Fairbanks Steam Shovel. While smaller than Marion Steam Shovel, Fairbanks Steam Shovel production lines ran at a steady pace during the company's existence. The Fairbanks Steam Shovel plant was located north of Marion Steam Shovel's plant, accessible from Leader Street. (Courtesy of the Marion County Historical Society.)

MARION OSGOOD MODEL 48. Founded in 1910 by A. E. Cheney as the Marion Shovel and Dredge Company, later renamed the Osgood Company, this company produced shovels, draglines, and cranes under the Osgood, Marion-Osgood, and General Excavator brand names. The company was acquired by Marion Power Shovel in 1955. Osgood Street and Cheney Avenue in Marion were named for the company located in the south end of Marion. (Courtesy of the Marion County Historical Society.)

MARION MODEL NO. 50. Photographed for Marion Steam Shovel's engineering department is this model No. 50 along the rail line connecting the main plant to the west Marion factory. This shovel was mounted to a railcar base with stabilizers, allowing the boom a 160-degree radius. The tower to the far right in the picture is the Davids Street School building. (Courtesy of the Marion County Historical Society.)

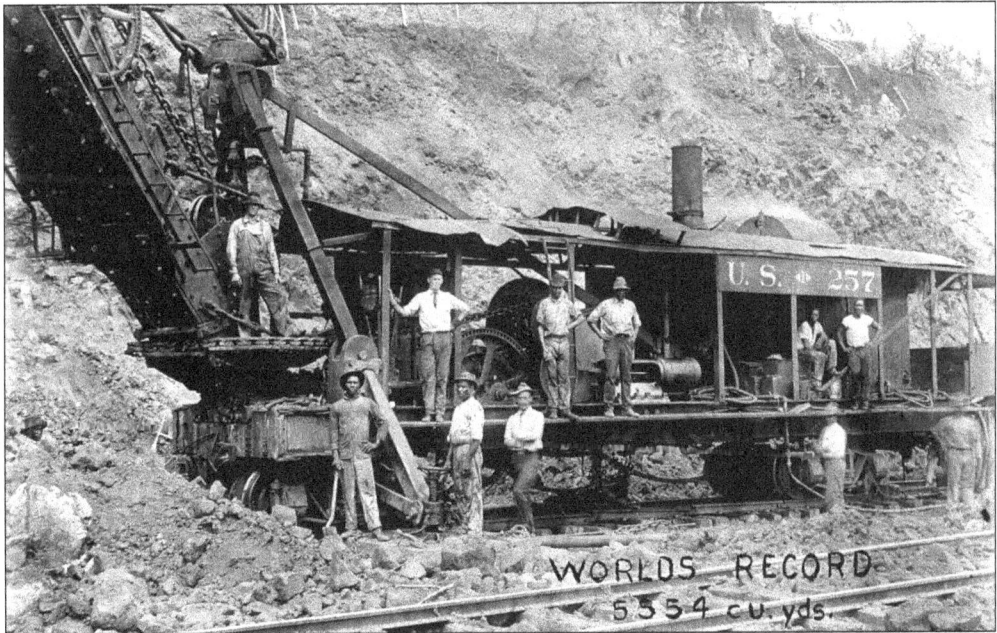

PANAMA CANAL CONSTRUCTION. Between 1902 and 1911, Marion Steam Shovel shipped 112 shovels to Panama for construction of what was the largest engineering project undertaken to date. While competitor shovels and draglines were also used on the project, Marion shovels consistently outlasted and outperformed the competitors and earned the records for amount of land cleared and heaviest loads lifted. (Courtesy of the Marion County Historical Society.)

MARION STEAM SHOVEL COMPANY, MAIN WORKS. This aerial image shows the scope of the Marion Steam Shovel Works main plant on Marion's west side, and its strategic position to the rail lines that run through the city. Many of the homes at the bottom of the image on Park Street and Olney Avenue were owned by Marion Steam Shovel employees. (Courtesy of the Marion County Historical Society.)

MARION STEAM SHOVEL, FROM KENTON AVENUE, AROUND 1934. Looking south from Kenton Avenue, this image not only shows the Marion Steam Shovel plant, but the businesses located around the plant, which served the workers and neighborhood families. The small wooden shack at the railroad crossing housed the watchman, who monitored the tracks for oncoming trains. (Courtesy of the Marion County Historical Society.)

MARION STEAM SHOVEL OFFICE WORKERS, COMPANY PICNIC, 1935. While Marion's shovel industry employed thousands of men on the production lines and in engineering and management positions before World War II, women played an important role in the company as supervisors, clerks, and secretaries in the administrative offices by keeping the company's billing, accounting, and administrative support functions operating. (Courtesy of the Marion County Historical Society.)

AN OSGOOD MILESTONE, AROUND 1940. Under contract with the U.S. Army Corp of Engineers, Osgood produced its 1,000th model 200 shovel. Osgood employees and U.S. Army Corp of Engineers officials, along with the Harding High School marching band, were on hand for the ceremonies. (Courtesy of the Marion County Historical Society.)

THE MOUNTAINEER. In 1955, Hanna Coal Company commissioned the Mountaineer, the largest traction land shovel in the world. With a 65-cubic-yard bucket, the machine also incorporated an elevator for its operators in its center pin. Though retired, the Mountaineer is still located in eastern Ohio, near the city of Cadiz. (Courtesy of the Marion County Historical Society.)

NASA CRAWLER, 1967. In the 1960s, NASA awarded Marion Power Shovel the contract to design and build a "crawler" that would transport the agency's Gemini and Apollo rockets and space shuttles from the hangar to the launch site. This image was taken in Florida where the machines were assembled. In 2007, NASA celebrated the 40th anniversary of the Marion Power Shovel–built crawler. As a testament to its design and build quality, NASA has no immediate plans to replace it. (Courtesy of Craig Barnhart, Gary Barnhart collection.)

Visit us at
arcadiapublishing.com